WHOLESOME WHOLE POETRY

J. Eileen

Langaa Research & Publishing CIG
Mankon, Bamenda

Publisher

Langaa RPCIG
Langaa Research & Publishing Common Initiative Group
P.O. Box 902 Mankon
Bamenda
North West Region
Cameroon
Langaagrp@gmail.com
www.langaa-rpcig.net

Distributed in and outside N. America by
African Books Collective
orders@africanbookscollective.com
www.africanbookscollective.com

ISBN-10: 9956-550-82-5

ISBN-13: 978-9956-550-82-1

Table of Contents

I. Mind

II. Body

II. Spirit

I
MIND

if i touch u

if i touch u
will it cause u 2 break
for your heart to unfold
inviting me into a world full of memories
will they overshadow the touch of my hand
or kiss of my lips

if i touch u
will it remind u where u r, have been & want to be
walking between all 3

if i touch u
i'm touching me
awakening – stirring – passions & desires
laid to rest
but desperate to revisit, revamp and revision
especially walking the halls in the middle of heaven and
hell translating stories

if i touch u
will it cause u 2 pause
even when duty calls
will the longings of my spoken and
silent screams be heard
in the midst of your world
your walls
even i as strong as i am want to be rescued
to be the damsel in distress

but my own history informs me to run
far away from u
but still i press

if i touch u
will u risk urself
to walk with me ~ as my lover friend
i c me n u
trying to reconcile life
and live congruently

if i touch u
what will u really do?

To Love

To love-
        Standing naked hand in hand
                Side by side
Baring our souls
Unveils the rawness of who we are

While we commune in a sacred space
                a liminal space
                a state in which time cannot be
                counted or kept

Our feelings are handled with kid gloves
            and listened to, with the ears of our
hearts

The message of sincerity and truthfulness
        of two souls beat in syncopation
Strong and steady, received and cradled with care

Slowly easing the pain of the past

Standing Naked
            With arms and hearts open wide
To each other
For each other
            Waiting-Yearning-Hoping-Praying
                That our individual
souls will bond

And become one, strong together
                              and away from ourselves

        Breathing life,
Letting none nor anything come between us

            Standing side by side
                    Hand in hand
            Walking together

            Holding each other close…

Loving You

Loving You
is like watching the dawn of a new day being born

You bring peace to my soul

Loving You
is like loving the most tender part of my very own heart
and soul

I treasure you

Loving You
is understanding your implicit words

I listen quietly and intently to you

Loving You
is feeling the warmth of the sun on my face
as well as being blanketed under the midnight sky

I am enraptured by the essence of you

I love you

Inexplicable Love

He is whom i want
>To walk with •
>To dream with
>To share my life with
>To share an eternity with

My heart flutters at the very sound of His voice
My body craves His touch

His love is my Desire
i too am the Shulamite Bride who, to her groom, says:
"kiss me again and again for your love is
"sweeter than wine which intoxicates my soul!"

His love surrounds me
>Engulfs me
>Overshadows me
>And overtakes me

And encourages my heart to try again
>To strive again
>To beat again

His love for me is a breeze and the fragrance of a rose

I too sing His praises to all who will listen
>Have you seen him?

he is ~~the~~ dark and dazzling - a midsummer night dream
his skin has been painted stroke by stroke midnight
black, dark chocolate brown by the West African sun

8

his lips and kisses are Ogbunike mango sweet!

he is a mighty warrior
standing Empire State Building tall

Have you seen him?
he is all that i want
he is dark and dazzling
his eyes are summer moon round and bright
And from his heart radiates love for me

This love for me is inexplicable!
It's even a mystery to me!

Because I Love You

Because I Love You –
I will steal away to you like a jealous lover
And reveal myself to you
I will open my heart and tell you my dreams
As I hold you in my arms until the dawn of a new day
comes

Because I Love You –
I will find my way to you in the darkest of the midnight
hour
Even when there is no gleam of hope – from the
midnight sky –
Not even one single beam of moonlight to lead me to
you
I will just stop and listen –
For the faintest cry from you or the slightest beat of
your heart
I know you anywhere

Because I Love You –
I adore you – I let everyone go for you
No one can compare to you
You love me like no other
If I am away from you for just one moment –
My heart aches for you

Because I Love You –
I will follow you until the end of time

In your arms is where I want to be
In your arms is where I want to die
No matter what people say
I will live my life your way

I adore you
There is no one else like you
I will steal away to you

A Whisper in The Wind

This whisper in the wind
Sometimes catches me in the breeze of you

Swept away in the coolness of your words
And enraptured by the touch of you

Like a tree in the wind, I bend from extreme to
extreme
Lost to the rapture –
But at times ready to leave you

A breeze cannot change –
Anything can make it change
From a soft cool breeze to a violent storm
How unpredictable!

Just like you and I

Like a whisper in the wind
The words we exchange get lost or forgotten
But if heard – are they really listened to?

This whisper in the wind
Sometimes catches me in the breeze of you

Yearning

I long for the sweetness of life
to live with a heart extended towards the heavens ~
and dance to
the beat of my lover's heart

I yearn for the sweetness of life
to live a life of bountiful possibilities
to actualize dreams deferred and
feel the pulse and heartbeat of my own

I yearn for the sweetness of life
to listen to live music on the green and
eat from the basket of joy and laughter

I yearn for the sweetness of life
to reconnect with friends of old
who have gone away and
disappeared into the oblivious gray of life

I yearn for the sweetness of life
to obtain the impossible dream
that vaporizes into thin air

Who will rescue me from the miserableness of life~
and hold me in my own sufferings

Longing for You

I hear your voice in the stillness of the night
like faint whispers in the wind
that ripple over, across and through my mind's eye
as my spirit sometimes screams like the
crescendoing howl of a hyena in the midnight hour

afraid and alone in the darkness

I cleave to the memory of you
clenching thoughts of you close to my chest
when I need you the most
even though now – you are but a dream
as different shades of your shadow
dance across my pillow under the moon lit sky

I reach out to touch you – once again but
you slip through my fingertips like the breath I breathe
you are spirit
like the air that rearranges the heavens
like the breeze that blows leaves
like the storms that torment the seas
then wreak havoc upon the land, just like the landscape
of my mind

I miss you in ways unimaginable
In which words cannot articulate –
The unfathomable depth and breadth of emptiness
In me concern you

I often wonder is there, will there ever be comfort for
me again
knowing I am alone without you

Then suddenly – hope flats from the depth of my soul
to remind me
That one day I will see you again
One day I will hold you again
One day I will be free again
Because I will be with you

Loud Silence

The silence is too loud
The stillness is too busy
Still behind the 8 ball
Standing on shaky ground
Living on borrowed time
Facing my own mortality in the mirror
My knowingness is meaningless

Chewing and choking on the cud of shattered dreams
That cut like glass
Hard to swallow blood and tears
Hard to swallow meaningless years
Hard to swallow bitter tears
Hard to swallow life

The silence is too loud
The stillness is too busy
My words are too heavy to shove across my tongue
My words are too dense to cut with a silver spoon
My words are buried underneath the dark center of this
dark soul

Not a sound can rise and give life to my thoughts
My thoughts that don't make sense to an outsider
My thoughts carry the dead bodies
My thoughts carry my dead body
My thoughts carry a cold heart
My thoughts are not separate from me

My thoughts are me

Don't bury me
Carry me to a place of rest
Carry me to a place of love
Carry me for I'm not strong
Carry me for I am weak
And tired of holding on

I'm weary
I'm empty
I'm broken
I'm frail not in appearance
I'm frail not in body
I'm frail not in spirit
I'm tender in heart
The filter is gone
The filter was shattered
I'm tired of talking

The silence is too loud
The stillness is too busy
I'm tired of being strong

Midnight Lover

Midnight lover
I meet you
At my window pain

Confronted with feelings
I've laid to rest
And
Promises I wish to forget

I stand
Touching the glass of my heart
My window

Quickly
I run and hide
And leave the window unlocked

I feel you
Close to me
Touching me
In intimate places

Holding me

I whisper your name
Praying you won't hear
Praying you won't stop
Praying you'll leave me

Here in the darkness of my room

In your arms
I relax
Telling you all my secrets
That spill from my soul

Tears fall
In disbelief
Of how much I really need you
Of how much I really care
Of how much I really do love you

Leave me here
To die alone
I don't want to need you
Not for another night

Let my heart rest
And anticipate its death

Please ~
Midnight Lover
I beg you
To leave me alone
Quickly flee
As you have come
Into my room

Loving me wholly
Completely

You make me give to you

Shatter the glass
In my window
Leave me the pieces
So, I can cut my own heart

Let's sever all ties
I can see
My way through the darkness
I can find my way out

Please
Midnight Lover
Leave me alone

Shadow Wrestling

Wrestling with shadows
from the cavernous abyss
of memory lane, the deep groans shriek!

Haunted~ jilted ~ traumatized by the depressive gloom
overpowering and overwhelming the sensibility
jumping blindly in the dark
flailing about from the walls of each memory
contained in a safe place
under lock and key
only to be entangled in the intricacies
of the fine lines of the brain freeways to the heart
of invisible silk strings
or the elaborate, elastic spider's web

Entrapped with the shadows ~ clobbered by fear
trying not to succumb to the deluge of anxiety that
rides high ~
drowning all life

Scrambling to find higher ground
cutting, pushing, defending what little peace of my soul
is left

Silence is golden
especially when the shrills from my heart rings loud in
my ears

The body remembers, it will never forget
each battle scar that was carved into the skin of my
memory with a dull knife

The body remembers each jagged edge word
that chomped at the wound~ infecting it ~ making it
blister, bubble and bleed

My soul remembers ~ the invisible wounds I carry
that hurt the most
keloid scars from memory lane
that are wrapped around the chambers of this beating
heart
extending octopi like tentacles to other vital organs

I've died this death a thousand times over –
only to be resuscitated back to life
To live again

Hold Me

Hold me during the darkest part of the midnight hour
stand watch over my soul while i breathe
it is here i encounter death
and face my fears

Hold me during the darkest part of the midnight hour
as you watch the tears fall
collect them for me in a glass jar
each tear has a story ~ one day they will speak

Hold me during the darkest part of the midnight hour
boldly speak peace over my troubled soul~
all that you feel
all that you hear
all that you discern

Keep my secrets close to your chest

Hold me during the darkest part of the midnight hour
until my eyes open
and i rise from the battle
surviving one more night
to walk into the dawn

Surrender

In the stillness
Ensconced by the black midnight sky
      The full moon wanes in the center
Glowing, illuminating the dark shadows that surround my
heart and soul

I sit there until the morning calm breaks as the dew
rests on my soul
With my head and heart in hand left traumatized

But still… Secretly I'm filled with hope

Heavy with uncertainty and hopeful for new beginnings
      My heart begins to speak with my mind
      As my mind speaks to my spirit
      As my spirit speaks to my creator

All one voice, in unison- longing
Praying for the same thing
Believing for the same thing

Tears erupt from the dark dank abyss of my soul
      A place where the flame of hope
And faith had been choked out by years of
disappointment and broken promises

I sit under the heavenly skies as raw emotions
      Gut wrenching soul sobs shake

Allowing the true condition of my being to be exposed
     Vulnerable and Afraid
        In love and loved
           Alone and lonesome, lonely

I clench life
Trying to stay connected with the dream that is etched
across my heart by my Creator's hand
I remember each pen stroke
Like a scalpel that cuts across the flesh of my heart as
blood dripped like tiny tears
Only to dry in the grooves of each letter

Reminding me of the sacrifice that was already made
Leaving my soul to ache
Oh! How my soul hurts and nothing can take the pain
away

Still… I sit and pray
With the essence of my being exposed
like a wounded warrior left in the trenches surrounded
by the enemy

I wave the white flag of surrender

Morning

It's a fresh morning
I have paused to breathe deeply
I stopped to exhale

Fresh rain falls slowly
From the heavens to the earth
Washing over me

The wind blows gently
Peace is surrounding the earth
I can relax now

I have tuned out noise
Peace fights to rise within me
I fight to breathe now

I fight to live now
I fight the demons again
I fight to breathe now

Fresh wind fresh fire
I question the God I know
I weep deeply bruised

Dream Again

In the quiet stillness of the night
During the calm of the morning
In the tranquil center of self

Suspended between heaven and hell
Hidden securely in the presence of my God
The doors of my heart are unfurled
As my heart speaks openly and candidly unveiling the
mysteries of its mind and soul
To the Creator of heaven and hell
Light and darkness
Water and earth
Birds and beasts
Man and woman

I hear a soft gentle voice speak with resounding clarity
and ask
What does your heart and soul truly desire that your
mouth dare not speak?

Overwhelmed by,
In awe of,
'n
Enraptured by God's presence
My mouth quivers
As jumbled stammering words tumble off my tongue
fighting to be heard

While tears spring forth from the bosom of my soul
and spill over my cheeks
While I lay prostrate before my Lord cloaked in
humility

A perfect peace falls over me
Like dew on the morning grass
I hear a soft gentle voice whisper to my soul repeatedly
Dream Again
I dare you to dream the unimaginable
And allow the meditations of your heart intertwine with
mine

Dream Again
I dare you to dream the unspeakable
The hidden treasure of your heart
That you locked away and tucked back in the corners
of your mind

Dream Again
I dare you to dream the impossible
And allow me to weave your dream
Which is my dream like the skilled artisan in the market
waiting for the right buyer

Dream Again
I dare you to live

In the quiet stillness of the night during the calm of the
morning
In the tranquil center of self

Peace is my portion
Here I dare to dream again
Here I dare to live

Again .... I Wonder

I wonder
What you dream
And what your heart tells your spirit
And what your spirit whispers into God's ears

If only I could hear you

I wonder
What hidden desire lights the flame of hope in your
heart

If only I could be near you

I wonder
If you reach for me while your mind
And spirit transcend the physical...
Only to realize that it was all a dream

If only I can touch you

I wonder
Whose name you call right as, or before, dawn kisses
The horizon and your eyes search the heavens for
God's tender mercies

If only you could hear my prayers

The Hope of Love

The hope of love stirs my heart,
awakens dreams buried in the midst of life's drama
which caused hope to shrink, shrivel and slither to a
safe place within my soul

This hope of new possibilities awakens
the soul to rise again,
to believe yet again in the impossible dream that faded
to black
and disappeared into the busyness of the canvas of
survival

The hope to breathe again the deep breaths which once
filled my lungs with
life…
the ruah of God
sustains me
but it felt as if I was suckered punched in the belly
which left me doubled over looking at the ground
gasping for air
trying to regain life and the breadth of God…

The hope of love has opens my mind's eye
and makes me see again past the emptiness of the gray
scale of life
which had left me color blind and in the dark
clinging to the invisibleness of God
- who whispers in the ear of my heart

to resuscitate life

The hope of love
has returned to me,
filled with dreams awaiting
birthing, to breathe and speak to me again

What Happened?

What happened to the dreams of my heart?
The place where I thought all was possible
The well of hope was full
But hope deferred makes the heart sick
And my heart has been, for years, a cancer patient
Eaten up by a dis – ease
So, has my heart
Unleavened dreams
Unleavened life
Unleavened hope
Deflated faith
Hopeless almost unto death
Death has overshadowed me
Placing its dark hand over my mouth and nose

Bitter Sweet

Life is bitter sweet, far from the honey I dreamed of as
a small girl,
The hopeless romantic who believed in the power of
love and all it could offer

Life is bitter sweet
As a more mature girl
I won't yet call myself a woman
I don't think I've accomplished any womanly things,
by no fault of my own
Which has filled my cup with bitter tea
So, I pour it to the ground
As a libation to honor the past....

Life is bitter sweet
As I search for the tangible things to hold in my hands
that will bring joy to my heart
and push the sweetness of life to return to me

My Greatest Sorrow

My greatest sorrow
Not waking up to you every morning
And whispering Good morning to you as I gently
caress your face

My greatest sorrow
Not being able to love you every day and showing you
the tenderness of my heart
As I unveil the dreams of my heart

My greatest sorrow
Not being able to talk with my children every day and
demonstrate the true power women possess

My greatest sorrow
Not being able to celebrate life with you
With all the plans we made and all the uncertainties

My greatest sorrow
My heart aches from missing you

The Courage to Believe

Heaven held me in her arms as I slept under the
darkness of the midnight sky
She whispered a word in my ear
Take hold of courage and believe again

She rocked me in her arms and sang a lullaby to me
Reassuring me of all the dreams
Unspoken and dreams yet to be

Heaven held me in her arms as I slept under the velvety
midnight sky
Clearly, I heard a booming voice speak to me, piercing
and shaking the stars

It takes courage to believe and stand face to face with
adversity and stare back into its unrelenting eyes
It takes courage not to lose focus or tuck tail and run
and hide
while blocking out all of the negative words that sting
like venom which spew from its hot volcanic mouth

Oh, how heaven held me in her arms and rocked me
until I eased back to sleep

Heaven held me in her arms as I laid naked under the
midnight sky
A face appeared to me in my dreams and spoke words
of wisdom like only a mother could

Take hold of courage and wear it like a knight wears
armor in battle and wield the sword like a dagger
bludgeoning all who come to kill your dream
Hold fast like your ancestors and call on your God,
moving your God to act swiftly upon your behalf
Dig deep and hold high the flag of righteous
indignation and wave it for all to see
Let it burn with hope bringing life back to you

Heaven held me in her arms
As she carried me over the threshold from fear to
courage and showed me the promised land where I saw
the desires of my heart materialize and leave a legacy

New Beginnings

New Beginnings
Once haunted by old memories from the past
Still my heart aches for more,
yearning for the impossible dream filled with endless
hope, with endless life,
with endless love

I begin each new day with a supplication in my heart
That stirs the dregs of faith, causing words to rise from
the shores of my soul, to dribble in, spill over my lips
and flow to the heavens
Capturing the attention of the lover of my soul

I feel peace surround me

Ensconced,
Enraptured by my lover's presence my heart hopes
again
For what I thought I lost
For what I thought I could never have
For what I thought I could never hold

It is in the New Beginning
That I have found myself
Clearly defined
Ever striving to be for me first and then you
I am unashamed of who I am
I have overcome the despair that almost killed me

That almost snuffed out my dreams

But I held on for dear life
In the midst of the struggle
In the midst of the fire
In the midst of the pain

The true meaning of love, life. and hope have been
restored
Have been regained

New beginnings
I begin each new day with a prayer in my heart
That whisks my faith, gives me hope, gives me courage
to love again

II
BODY

Throw Caution

Throw caution to wind and come to me.
Steal away from the busyness of life
Lay your head upon my breast and find comfort in my
arms
Allow me to hold you during the darkest of the
midnight hour
until dawn breaks and dreams are restored
Fear not - taste the sweetness of my lips; drink life
from my breasts
While I speak kind words to your heart of hearts

O' come and lay your head upon my breast and listen
to the beat of my heart while we share dreams and
thoughts with each other
Speak to me in the darkest of the midnight hour until
sunrise
Until my eyes are heavy and my soul is at ease to rest in
the strength of you
Find it not strange that I steal kisses from your lips
while I meditate upon the horizon
My heart's desires....

O' Come and lay your head upon my breast until we
are both restored

i Simply Like

i simply like the sound of your voice
and the way the words you speak
roll across your tongue and cascade down
the fullness of your lips
like a soft kiss
i wish to taste

i simply like the cadence of your voice
and how it reverberates through the line….
wrapping around me like a warm winter sweater;
cozy and soft making
me drift off to sleep

i simply like your Louisiana drawl
which drips slow like molasses on a warm breakfast
plate
i sop you up with a biscuit to eat…
then lick my fingers to remove the sticky sweetness
the way i imagine you to be

i just simply like you

Dark and Dazzling

You are a dark and dazzling summer's midnight sky
kissed by moonlight. The same sky under which lovers
lose themselves– wrapped, tangled, and tied by passion
Until their insatiable hunger is met.

Ooey Gooey Sticky Chewy Kinda Love

I want that ooey gooey sticky chewy kinda love
That finger lickin lip smackin kinda love
That makes you want more
Till your tummy is too tight could pop kinda love

I want that ooey gooey sticky chewy kinda love
That spine tingling can't get enough of that kind of
love
Can't catch your breath
Toe curling kinda love
That love that everyone sees from afar
And wishes that she had who you have
But his eyes are only for you kinda love

I want that ooey gooey sticky chewy kinda love
Where he leaves off you finish
Where she leaves off he finishes
That kinda love that makes you wanna be more than
you ever thought you could be
So he can see how much you mean to him
So she can see how much you love her unconditionally
So all can see the light that you share

I want that ooey gooey sticky chewy kinda love
That makes my heart flutter from the sound of his
voice kinda love
That makes your heart flutter from the sound of my
voice kinda love

Where the smell of my sweet perfume inebriates him
and takes him back to the place of ecstasy
Where the smell of his cologne takes me back to that
back scratchin' deep slow grindin place
The place where we share paradise kinda love

I want that ooey gooey sticky chewy kinda love
That toe tappin' hand clappin kinda love
That makes you bow down and pray
And rise up and rejoice
That bluesy soulful kinda love
That makes you wanna slow dance and listen to love
songs all day and night long kinda love

I want that ooey gooey sticky chewy kinda love
That sweet bubble gum kinda love
That makes you chew until your jaws are tight and the
flavor is gone kinda love
Where you blow big bubbles and pop your gum kinda
love
That loud pop that makes your mama or your close
friends tell you to stop chewin' your gum like that
kinda love
I want that ooey gooey sticky chewy kinda love
That makes you wanna call off work kinda love
That makes you wanna layup kinda love
Where there are no inhibitions
But movies and pillow talk kinda love

I just want that ooey gooey sticky chewy kinda love

Phone Sex

In the dark
In the chair
Legs spread wide
Receiver held to my lips
I whisper words
Into the line
Telling things divine
I hear your voice
Speaking softly
Shallow breaths
And little moans
I touch you
Touch me
Holding your penis in my hand
Touching my clit
Close to my lips
I breathe
On your head
Breathe on mine
Hot throb
I tickle the tip
With my tongue
Slow wet drip
Warm
Tingles up my spine
I lean back
And relax
Pulling you closer

Feeling you
Feeling me
Caressing my breasts
Playing with my nipples
Taut
Sweat comes down
I feel your passion
My passion
Moan – Cry
Legs wider
Inside
Sticky sweet
Shooting off
Slow wet drip
Cum

The Kiss

He kissed my lips as if he owned them,
making love to them – teasing them
with his tongue and light nibbles of
his teeth while lightly pulling…
and sucking – as if my clitoris was in his mouth…

Moist, resisting the temptation to succumb to the roller
coaster
of his passion
i whispered pleadingly into the darkness of the room….
no

Not ignoring the faint breath of my word…
He pulled me closer caressing the exposed parts of my
nakedness
underneath my tee shirt and resigned himself to the
other bed

Slightly disappointed and relieved at the same time…
hoping he would ignore my request; seducing me to
give in.
i appreciated his gentleness which in this moment
spoke volumes louder than the seductive act of kissing

Awakened by The Midnight Storm

Awakened by The Midnight Storm
     You are lying next to me
I can only see your naked silhouette
     As flashes of lightening shines through the
window

Brightening up the sky

I roll closer to you
     Feeling the warmth of your body next to mine

As the claps of thunder become louder
     I hide in the warmth of your arms
Laying my head on your chest
     Listening to your heart
I close my eyes trying to imagine what you are
dreaming of

I cannot
     Instead, my imagination gets the best of me

Carefully –
     I roll away from you
Taking my clothes off – Studying every curve of your
body

Drinking you in – inch by inch

I go over to you
>
> Lightly pressing my taut breasts against yours

Letting the rest of me melt into you

I let my tongue trace the softness of your lips

Lifting up slightly
>
> Like the stormy wind blows through the trees

I rearrange myself
>
> I let my fingertips touch you
>
> Tracing the curve of your muscular arms
>
> Tickling your rippled stomach
>
> Even teasing your nipples

I let my tongue do the rest

I gently slide down

Making a trail from head to head

I stop
>
> Lingering for only a moment

A flash of lightning bolts through the sky

I hold you in the palm of my hand
>
> Feeling you throb with excitement

I get you wet

Plunging you in a deep puddle

Sucking you in like a tornado
You are lost in the eye of my storm

Beads of sweat roll from you
        Like the rain falls from the sky
Fast and Steady
        You are floating – high above any cloud
You tremble and shake
        Worse than any earthquake

You hold on for dear life to the edge of the bed
        But your grip is not tight enough
Only I can keep you up

The storm is over
        And your climatic moment is upon us
You shoot off like a falling star
        With beads of sweat upon your head

You sit up- Dazed

Trying to figure out if you were really dreaming
        Or if you were Awakened by My Midnight
Storm

Silent Acquiescence

He's different now
> Or is it just me?

There is a gentleness about him
> a peacefulness
> a silent acquiescence that speaks volumes of his
heart's desires,
 what his mouth dares not speak

I have the right to interpret him
> We've been lover friends for over 14 years
Not consecutive years, but years that taper off and
begin again

There isn't anything he doesn't know about me
> Except the depth of feeling I have for him
But there is so much that I don't know about him
> Leaving my imagination to run wild to try to see
beyond the silence,
Opening the door to the silent emotion, to his actions
and miss actions

Every now and again
> The truth of his reality is spoken
Compounded by the complexities of life
> Living through the gray scale

I listen to, filter, sift, and meditate over his spoken
word
> It's so easy to be drawn into the raw emotion of
him

This yearning for wholeness, peace and unconditional
love
   Rejecting
    Mocking
The invitation to love only me
   Weeping
Pouring salt, while stabbing his ego
 Wedging a brooding hurt
 like an infected
Paper cut, across the top of my heart, which caused me
to slam the doors shut

Suddenly and unexpectedly,
   After years of silence, my whole being is
thrown into crisis
I am depleted, sucked dry of emotion and spirit, only a
shell of a woman remains

My life hangs 'twixt and 'tween life and death,
   Heaven and hell,
   Sanity and insanity,
   Faith and hopelessness,
I call him, summon him with despair
   He's never heard me like this before
Usually I am fierce and strong
But in this moment, I am broken, and I need my lover
friend
Before I could even muster courage or even ask him to
meet me somewhere,
   Anywhere, he was there; I was nervous with
anxiety…

We didn't say much

for hours on end I wept silently in his arms
with him kissing and caressing me back to life;
chasing rigor mortis till blood pumped through every
vein

I feel myself breathe again as memories come rushing
in
I remember what it is like, to have him like this,
passionate,
attentive, tender, in tune with all my silent
acquiescence's
All my needs and wants met in the moment
The tidal waves of passion billowing over the banks of
my heart
Rinsing away the debris of the past, cleansing
the paper cut of my soul
With the sting still there

Trying to enter, the doors will not open
His eyes flash with anger, speaking with a
controlled roar,
Not meant for me – but for her – the other woman
Who seduced him with lies and deceit
My face - blank as my heart sinks, and the bridge to my
being is
lifted, and locked again

Turning my face to the wall to hide my pain
calling my name, refusing to answer, he walks out the
door
Rising with indignation and overwhelming sadness
locking the door once more- screaming expletives,
drowning in bitter tears,

shaking my tiny fist in protest, violently jerking my body
about the room
sliding down the cool hard wall that stills and cools the
explosive
fire that burns
silence rushes in engulfs me until the migraine and
blood shot eyes dissipate

He's different now
       or is it just me?

I invited him over to seduce,
       to tease
       to tickle my fancy

His divorce is final,
       and my mind dances back and forth:
wanting him for myself or leaving things the way they
are
       as silent acquiescence's

There he is, body buck naked, soul exposed, with silent
desires and screams
       covering him as I walk up the stairs to retrieve
the lotion,
the only barrier between us

I rest beside him
       sitting crisscross apple sauce shaking the bottle

drizzling the cold contents across his skin
       He breathes in deeply and lightly, blows out
while he flinches and shivers

the warmth of my hand eases and erases the chill and
apprehension that slightly exists

massaging fire of passion in circular motions
finger walking down his spine, thick and strong back,
gliding over his buttocks, kneading the back of his
hamstring, allowing the tentacles of heat to
            reach into his inner thigh, brushing against his
jewels
while listening for him to say something
        But nothing escapes his mouth, only a silent
acquiescence

He flips over,
            Resting on his elbow, flashing a devious smile,
motioning with his eyes to look below
showing me his pulsating desire - inviting me for a ride
while still making long strokes down his legs
and pushing the stress through his toes to resist
temptation

The massage is over
            Resting,
        Wrapping his limbs around me
his hand disappears behind the veil and eases its way to
my breast, gently caressing
        the other screams to be touched too
Pressing his face, a little closer to the back of my neck
            feeling his hot breath as his chest rises and falls
Pulling me closer, lifting me out of clothes protesting
with a slight giggle and a brief stiffening of the body -
enjoying the warmth of his mouth
            roaming

tossed in the river of wetness shaking,
inhaling deeply
exhaling slowly,
searching for words
 thoughts ricocheting

I only hear silent acquiescence whispering

pausing

TAKE ME! RAVISH ME! CONSUME ME!
ENTER ME!

Encircling his body around mine
        like a snake does a tree
feeling the warmth of his skin,
the warmth of his arms,
the softness of his cheek pressed to mine

My eyes close gently
while losing myself
        Praying

Just a gentle glide
        a parting of the door as he crosses the
threshold
meeting him with my passion
        pushing back to rise and fall to him
moans escape me
        I hear his desire
feeling the intensity of the dialogue
as it plays with all the what if's? and why shouldn't I's?

breathing him in slowly like a sip on a straw of a slow
gin fizz

       Inebriating

He's different now
       or is it just me?

Woman-Mother-Me

As a woman
I am like no other
My body's made to hold life
To nurture nations
To heal the wounded

My hips set wide
Like my stance
I squat with my head
Tilted towards the heavens
Screaming to the high heavens
As my womb
Cradles life within
Forcefully,
But gently expelling the fruits of my labor

Tears roll
From my eyes
Like sweat pours from my body
As my breasts leak
The sweet nectar
Children come and suckle
And listen
To the words of my mouth
That feed their hearts and souls

Full
They slumber peacefully
Like angels
As I watch over them
With a quick eye
I lay back to rest
And let my heart listen to their dreams
And protect their innocent hearts
That knows no pain

I rise quickly
On a moment's notice
And walk before them
To help guide them
To protect them from the hell that awaits

I open my mouth
to summon the angels on high
And whisper words of grace, wisdom, and protection
For my children

I dare not speak loudly
For fear of awakening them

I quickly return
Stroking each cheek
Listening to their every breath
Tenderly looking at the life that came from me

I lay back
And relax
And let my eyes close
But never
Do I close my heart.

Cocktail

Betrayed by the heavens and the earth
Made in the image of God
Taken from the rib of Adam
Molded from the clay of the earth
Surrounded by mirrored images

But still... I am...
Almost to the point of death

The voice of my uterus bleeds angrily in protest from
all that she has tried to accomplish
Gnashing teeth on the aborted dreams or miscarried
relationships
Familiar hands have entered into the depths of her -
that touch one way as if in love -secretly
Hiding a straight razor that cuts with venomous
control, conceit, and fear

I didn't live my life in stir ups with my bottom pushed
down to the edge of the table
Instead, I kept her close to dwell deep within to be
cradled by the warmth of the pelvic palace
Now she wears her own crown
A crown made of knotted scars which remind her of
the finiteness of life desperately,
Fearfully wanting to beat the clock that ticks loud
within the ears of her heart and soul

Grieving the lives that have been stolen
I work twice as hard to stay present
In the here and now~ and not climb deep within
The silent world of my walls

As I hang in the balance
The liminal space
Where heaven and hell meet
I leave myself- to journey to a space
Where I take the inner chambers of my heart and open
wide
The doors of my spirit to read the promises that are
etched
Across my heart by my Lover's hands

Here in the garden where I hoped to find peace
I am tormented by each promise
Hope deferred has sickened the depths of my being
As flashes of others who have done less
or nothing at all come before me
mocking me ~like Pinnanah did Hannah
But there is no one there to ask me if he is enough?
To satisfy that inner burning that has driven me to the
brink to take one last step
With my eyes clinched wide
When I hear the voice of my lover
Cry out to me
Calling me by my name
I turn slowly
With my Molotov cocktail of emotions
Laced with anger with the wick

Of disappointment burning – ready to explode in my
hands
I face life square on
As my inconsolable heart tries to find peace and
comfort

To Die of a Broken Heart

A dark gloomy cloud hovers over me
Smothering all the strength and life out of my body
Leaving me to lie lifeless

Gusts of winds blow
Bending trees as if they were rubber bands
Snapping them back – straight and taut

I cannot breathe

I gasp for air as acid rain falls from the sky
And tears pour out of my eyes
Burning – seeping into the core of my heart
oozing blood with each falling tear

A pool of blood collects

As I catch a quick glimpse of my reflection
Of how frail and pail I appear
A thick lumpy glob is expelled from the deep recesses
of my bowels
Reeking a putrid stench

I moan

Grabbing at the air
Praying to the heavens above with all of the strength
left in me

for someone to save me from this horrible death
As vultures circle above
Swiftly swooping down
Picking at the shell of my body
Pulling me apart
Exposing the little life I have left to the elements

I can no longer hold on
My heart beats one last time
tears stain my face and the vomitus stench of death
from a broken heart lingers in the air

Southern Majesty

I love the silky smoothness of the rainbow
of your coffee complexioned skin
bathed and rinsed underneath the Alabama sun
mixed with the heat of the earth,
the water droplets and sweat as it ascends to your brow
like beads of pearls & precious gems which roll like tiny
rain droplets
to the small of your back

You are the most beautiful and tastiest mud pie
which melts in my mouth
rich from the terrain embracing the secrets of creation
holding the wisdom of wealth in your hands

I like the fullness of your lips
they remind me of my forefathers who were kings
like the Egyptian Sphinx standing tall in the sand
that brush me tenderly – tasting me hungrily
honey sweet
desiring to be closer to you
to become as one with you
I hold the throttle of my passion
it is like liquid glass
hot, steamy, transparent, powerful, all encompassing
beauty of me for you
creation celebrates you
I celebrate you!

I like the warmth of your heart
the inner workings of your mind
that I want ~hope to~ need to understand
and hear with an open ear~ silent pleadings of the
quintessence
of your being that transcends the heavens
when the earth is asleep
and blanketed by the velvety midnight sky~

Begging your God ....
who is mine as well ...to move the heavens and the
earth
to stand tall and wide
to command the forces that be to stand at attention
and honor the royalty that resides
and resonates within you ~
within me ~
within us

Your prayers draw me like a bee to a honey comb
like a hummingbird to the nectar of day lilies
I cannot resist

I like the rod of integrity
that you carry which empowers you
to knock down all the obstacles ~
invisible walls
internal tapes
scars that have entangled your mind and body
external walls that stand 10 feet tall

70

cutting the red tape that tries to bind what is rightfully
yours~
all these that rise against you
not settling for the status quo
pushing beyond limiting boundaries ~
the earth must give way
and align with the heavens
it shall be and will be so

I love the warrior in you
the fighter who won't succumb to mediocrity
but demands excellence ~
taking life by force~
the bull by the horns and trampling on fears

Rise Your Majesty

III
SPIRIT

Kingdom

I search my soul
To no avail to find words to describe this pain that
engulfs me
And leaves my stomach tied in knots

I whimper
As truth digs deep into the bitter root of lies that have
laced my mind
Pierced my heart, and squeezed hope from my womb
Like invisible parasites eating away dead meat

As my mind is renewed
And the dead parts of my heart and arteries are
resuscitated

I pass the bitter roots and parasites through my bowels

As truth becomes my friend
I cling to only Him
My heart yearns to be one with Him after the young
Shulamite bride that yearned to be
With her husband

Overwrought with mixed emotions
I watch the world around me crumble, and die in vain
Chasing empty dreams, fulfilling false self-prophecies

The bitter vomit of lies swims in and out of their eyes,
ears, and hearts
Leaving trails of sticky putrid patches of death, as the
stench lingers in the air everywhere
The carcass has been and on everything it has touched

My soul wails and my spirit travails leaving my body
weak
And my spirit strong in the midst of death and
confusion

I pursue eternal matters
Kingdom truths-that have empowered and catapulted
my mortal body and spirit in the next paradigm

Freeing myself from all dead relationships
I have severed the tie that has tormented me for years,
and caused my family to scatter, and never to return

I made one last attempt as a daughter and a Priest to
repair the break;
But the crippled man chooses death and to live in
denial, and not to humble himself and ask for
forgiveness

Choked on anger mixed with pain, fear and frustration
An explosive cocktail that was handled with care
I blessed the mess and closed the door as I heard the
silent unbelief scream from his soul

I walked away in disgust and crumbled under the
heavens as rejection blanketed me
And tried to kill me

But in the midst of it all
I choose life
I choose truth
I choose Christ

Whisper a prayer for me

Look into the midnight sky
And gently whisper into the wind as it blows across
your face
Caressing the words that fall from your lips
That floats into God's ears burning them with pain
That you are relaying to Him that my soul feels

Ask Him to hold me close and not let me stray too far
But guide me and keep me on the right path

During the darkest of the midnight hour
When you are all alone

Whisper a prayer for me

Tilt your head toward the heavens
Asking God to help me get through each new day
The worry – The frustration
But most of all the loneliness
How I walk alone
I often pray to God myself to please ease my pain

Whisper a prayer for me

During the darkest of my midnight hour
When I lay awake and alone
Drowning in the tears
Ask him to wipe them away
And hold me in his arms as I fall asleep

Please ...

Whisper a prayer

for me

Of All the Things

Of all the things my heart yearns for
Of all the things that make my heart swell with delight
Of all the things that make my heart sing

One simple thing-
That has escaped me time after time
And left me bruised and often times broken
But still my heart hopes, believes, and even dreams

To share my life with the one
Who will treat me with gentle kindness
And gaze upon me with adoring eyes

Of all the things my heart hopes for
Of all the things my heart beats so passionately for
To hear the voice of my lover as he speaks to the core
of my soul
As the words from his mouth, which are the
meditations of his heart
Surround and enrapture my soul
Bringing life to me
Bringing love to me
Bringing peace to me

Of all the things that my mind's eye dwells upon and
even mulls over
Reflecting over the storms of my heart and gently
traces every scar with the
Fingertips of my memory, my emotions, and my soul
Remembering each tear that has welled up, poured
over, and washed over my heart

Still
I hope, and fervently pray for the one who will leave
me breathless
From each embrace
From each passionate kiss
From each tender moment that we've shared
The long walks
The long talks in the dark
The silent nights where no sounds could be heard
The bright days when only light and joy could exist

Of all the things my heart yearns for
Of all the things my heart beats so wildly and
passionately for

For one simple thing

Love

Love Me for A Lifetime

Love me for a lifetime
And promise you'll never leave

In the morning
Wake me with a kiss
And smile tenderly

Love me for a lifetime
And follow me on our journey

Place your hand in mine
And walk beside me
Never turning back

Love me for a lifetime
And dream dreams with me
Allow me to grant you your heart's desire

Please
Love me for a lifetime

Enraptured

Enraptured by the essence of you
I listen to your every unspoken word
And pray fervently to hear your voice

Allow me to speak to your heart of hearts

Close your eyes
lay your head upon my breast,
relax in the warmth of my arms
And let the words of my mouth,
And meditations of my heart
Invade, fill, and rest in the secret chambers of your
heart

The intent of my heart is pure

As I hold you in the warmth of my arms
Reveal to me the dreams of your heart
Show me the true condition of you
Play the melody of your song

Allow the essence of my soul to engulf
And intertwine with yours
As I speak to the bosom of your soul

Listen intently
And relax in the warmth of my love

Living on a Whisper of a Word

Living on a whisper of a word
One special word that is more like a promise
A promise that gently cradles and caresses my heart
Leaving my imaginations to run wild like an
uncontrollable fire which blazes through the forest

This word that rests in the bosom of my soul
Which generates a deep feeling of warmth that is
unexplainable
But the luminous glow can be seen by all

Living on a whisper of a word that is put forth with
much thought and sincerity
Like a subtle autumn breeze that blows a leaf from its
limb to earth
So are the shivers that go up my spine
Leaving me to stand unclothed
Baring all
The most intimate part of my being
My soul

The treasure chest of all my feelings and emotions that
shape me into who I am
The rawness of my character that holds secrets to my
very existence
The seed of life that at times may lay dormant or at
others may bloom into a beautiful flower
Or a kind word

That one special word that works miracles for even the
most impatient

Living on a whisper of a word
That one special word that gives me strength to
weather one more storm
No matter how gusty the winds may blow
Or even bitter cold the air may be
And to even overcome the obstacles that are
sometimes catapulted before me

Living on the whisper of one special word
Love

My Soul Sings

My soul sings a soft sultry moanin' blues
Sarah Vaugh lets from highs to lows as she croons,
whines over and raps around what was lost, and maybe
will ne'er be

My soul sings the blues in its deep husky
bass baritone voice of Billie Holliday
slurring inaudible groanings over pain endured
witnessing the depths of strange fruit
that hung from limbs of trees that were
knotted with hate, ripped with heart tissue
and bruised bones and tendons down to the white meat
where chips of my soul were broken off

Their blood cries out from the soil!

My Soul sings belting from its gut what it
wants like Etta James – who yelled
I want a love that lasts past Saturday Night!
that raw mixture of passionate emotion
causing the hairs on the back of my neck to stand and
applaud
the bluesy – soulful – rich R&B – that lulls and
electrifies the spirit!
to move, sway, dance or tap my toes
demanding what it wants
not gentle soft pleadings - to compromise

My soul laments with a tear stained face
like my sistah Jill Scott
pleading… to live and not die in her misery
of pain of disbelief and disenfranchisement
of what following the rules brings
knee bent and body bowed
broken with no core strength to even
pull my chin to my knees where the weight
of my heart is carried
in the center of my womb where life grows,
is birthed, nurtured and flows

My soul sings that old Negro Spiritual
Motherless Child
while standing in an open field heaping ashes upon my
head
wailing – though choked on sobs with blood shot eyes
sometimes I feel like a motherless child
a long way from home... in a foreign land without a
familiar face
No comfort… No place to call home
often times wondering – God do you really care?
Do you really see me?
this world… O' Lawd was not designed for me, I'm
almost gone….
with nothing left to give

My soul travails during the midnight hour
'twixt and 'tween
before dusk and dawn
doubled over in a fetal position

with the voice of Mahalia Jackson singing over my soul
–

trouble of this world assuring me soon I will be done with
the troubles of this world and I can
go home and live with my Lord

My soul is uneasy
like a clanging gong as it rolls from hope to hopelessness
grasping for that fine line of faith that invisible string
that keeps
My soul still
My heart at ease
And my mind bound together
Holding on to the Amazing Grace
while a particular song gently plays in the back drop of
my life…

It is well with my soul

My soul sings
My soul sings
My soul sings

Secret Place

in the secret place of my heart
i carry you,
i hold you during the midnight hour
when dusk and dawn kiss
to start a new day
to start a new beginning

it's here i pray for you
asking the lover of my soul
the One who knows all
the One who hears me when I cry
to heal your broken heart
to restore the unspoken dreams, you hide deep within
your soul
to restore hope, you lost in the bitter canvas of life

it's here in the secret place of my heart
where i love you
even though you hide from me
so i can't see you
sometimes i can't hear you
but i feel you just the same

it's in the secret place of my heart
where God hears me when i pray for you

Intimate Vulnerability

it is the deeper longings of your heart
the unspoken words of your heart
in which I long to hear
the thoughts you hold deep within
the abyss of your soul
the place you retreat to
and take out the desires you
have tucked away
and occasionally play peek – a boo with

i long to kiss the soul of you
and braid the warmth of my love with yours
as we sit in our lover's Paradise
and listen to the heartbeat of each other

i want to hold you in the midnight hour
when the dark sky masks all
that is underneath it
giving space for intimate vulnerability
while I taste the saltiness of your words
and the wounds of that burn from deep within
with the hopes to heal you
with the love that burns deep within me for you

if Only

if only i could wipe your tears
And bottle the pain of your heart
And send it to the sea of forgetfulness i would

if only i could hold you close to my breast
So, you could hear the beating of my heart
As i speak words of healing over your
Broken soul asking the angels to descend
From on high with the balm of Gilead i would

if only i could massage your heart with the love
I have for you that has never faded away
But lay locked in the secret place of my heart i would

Sweet Dreams

Sweet Dreams
May the peace of the Almighty gently hold you
While the comforting embrace of love surrounds you

Sweet Dreams
May the breath you breathe refresh your spirit
While the toxins of your soul are exhaled

Sweet Dreams
May you rise in the morning with a renewed
countenance
A countenance that reflects the Divine who held you
while you slept

From the Quiet Place of My Heart

From the Quiet Place of My Heart,
the center of all mysteries
From where all life flows
I pray a fervent prayer for a special soul

I come to life here
I die to myself here
I seek God's face here

Here –
In the quiet stillness of my heart
I search my soul
Leaving no stone unturned
No corner unswept
I walk quietly
Listening to the thoughts of my mind
Listening to the thoughts of my heart
I stop
I reflect
I don't like all I've seen
I don't' like all I've heard

Now –
From the Quiet Place of My Heart
I fall on bended knee and bow
Rejoicing in His glory
Rejoicing in the center of His heart

I lay my burdens down
The burdens of today that cause my heart to ache

Please don't let me bleed to death

Cleanse the wounds of my heart
Don't let them fester and run like open sores
But let a song flow from the pain

From the Quiet Place of My Heart
I drink the milk of life that restores my mind
That replenishes my spirit

Here –
In the quiet stillness of my heart
I come to life
Here I die to myself
As I seek God's face.

Listen ...

Listen ...
To the quiet

Feel the stillness in the room

Peace

Listen...
To the soft rumble
Feel the wind blow

Disturbance

Listen...
To the loud clap of thunder
Hear the gusty winds whistle

Storm

Listen...

Drumrolls of Thunder

Drumrolls of thunder in the distance
rumblings from the northwest horizon
like low groanings from the heavens
swelling like rolling tides
to a monsoon like state
only to shrink to soft moans
of the inner workings of my brain
as my thoughts zig-zag
colliding with the conscious state
my heart has been awakened to
while thunder marches across
the open plain of possibilities
to meet the bubbling vehement
gusts of winds as they tumble and push back
clashing in the core of the earth
like iron strikes iron
shaking the ground
rattling the bones of the dead

Pausing
I inhale deeply
to aerate my lungs, mind and spirit
to exhale the toxic waste and
it's fumes that have seeped into
the fertile soil of my inner self~
choking out dreams and visions

A deluge pours from Paradise
saturating the terrain of the very essence
of my being
cleansing me, even the hidden boroughs of sorrow,
despair, low expectations of others and agitation
anxiety that has gripped and left me awake, sometimes,
oftentimes days on end
being tossed to and from
thought to thought
while lamenting to the Lover of my soul
to rescue me from me
I want to be packed with peace, laughter, love, joy,
grace, mercy, and hope
so new seeds can be sown
germinated and harvested
hence new life can be birthed

Drumrolls of thunder in the distance
speaks volumes to the uneasiness of my spirit
leaving me unsettled
as thoughts ricochet from corner to corner
some speaking to fears
some speaking to the dreamy
place in the hidden chamber of my heart
a quiet space that I retreat
to in the chaos of life
where I can meditate
and hear what the Prince of Peace speaks to me
as He holds me in His arms
comforting and easing the burdens of my life
that sometimes I put upon myself

so as not to feel the loneliness
that gnaws away and nags at the aspirations....
the desires of my heart
sometimes leading me to wonder
I am a fool to believe in love
eternal bliss, which has been stolen from or escapes me
even before dejectedness was my food day and night
and I withered away like grass with a distended belly
filled with dry rot and worms

However, a flood from the celestial skies drowned out
the worms while washing away the dry rot
leaving the fleshy tender part of me
to feel and believe again

Quiet Stillness

There is a Quiet Stillness
That lives deep
Within the belly of every human being

A stillness
That can awake
The raging sea
Or
Soothe the beast
That dwells in the darkest heart

A stillness
With
A voice
Mightier and powerful
Than the heartbeat of any child

This stillness
Is the guiding force
To righteousness
That will carry on
Far beyond the years
Of the oldest man

This Quiet Stillness
Warms the coldest soul
And brings life
To the deadest of hearts

By gently breathing
In a soft easy rhythm

This Quiet Stillness
Lives deep
Within me

Comfort Abound

Betwixt and between
the midnight hour
and the dawn of a new day
when the world is at rest
and ensconced in peace

i pray
that when a deluge of emotion
overtakes your soul and leaves you spent

that the Great I AM
walks in and finds you in
that secret place
and when the Creator calls
you answer
while the Almighty embraces
you and speaks to the inconsolable child in you

i pray
that as the heavens unfurl
and the angels descend from on high
encircling you
the sweet melodious sounds
that drip like honey from
their lips help extinguish
the pain from within

On the Other Side of Tomorrow

On the Other Side of Tomorrow
As the sun rises – birthing the dawn of a new day
The moon lights the darkness of the midnight sky

I let my eyes rest on the horizon
As I look into the heavens as the thought of him walks
through my mind

Here –
Under the heavens
I petition my Lord,
the Lover of my soul
to guard my fragile heart
That holds so much strength,
though weak and desperate to be loved

Out of desperation, frustration, and anxiety
I lay spread eagle as the issues of my heart flows from
the bosom of my soul
Vomiting old memories
Puking unshed tears
I taste the bitterness from the belly of disappointment
Mixed with the sweetness of hope from my heart

I raise my scarred and tattered heart
And allow my Lord to touch it
To trace the keloid scars
To heal those broken places within me

On the Other Side Of Tomorrow
As the sun sets – covering me under the midnight sky
I think of him – as the sun rises and shines on his face
As the warm rays kiss his lips

I rest in the comfort of my Father's arms
And articulate to Him what my heart yearns for –
What my heart truly desires
I pray earnestly and fervently that he loves the Lord
And is a man after God's own heart
Who walks with integrity, yields to and obeys the voice
of the Lord

I pray, as I rest in the bosom of my Father's chest
And listen to the beat of His heart
That he loves me as Christ loves the church
That he will provide for me, nurture me, care for me,
and be patient with me

I pray, as I slumber in the warmth of my Father's arms
Engulfed in the essence of His presence that I am all
he's ever hoped for
All he's ever prayed for

And when he hears my voice, he feels the peace of the
Lord wash over him
And when he looks into my eyes – he sees the Spirit of
the Lord, which dwells within me

On the Other Side Of Tomorrow
As I petition my Lord

I pray that He blesses his coming in and his going out
I pray that he feels His presence just as I do

I pray....

    I pray....

        I pray....

On the Other Side of Tomorrow

Once More

'Tis in the silence of the day
The fleeting moment when peace and tranquility kiss
that my mind rests
While my heart pounds and aches reminding me of
what I am striving for

My mind and soul often wonder
If you understand the magnitude of sacrifice
That I make for you and our children; seen and unseen

Often times my soul aches at the obstacles that I face
And the fears that mock the dream I have hidden in the
bosom of my soul which my spirit hovers over...
Protecting... the dream that has kept the flame of hope
and faith lit
In the darkest of my moments when my life flashed
before me
And my body was wracked with gut wrenching pain
that no pill, person, or drink could soothe

Only hot tears washed over my soul; turning the open
wounds of my life
The salt burned.... Leaving keloid scars to remind me
of the pain endured
Never to forget even when I get to lay my eyes on you
and touch you once again
To hold you in my arms....

To feel the tenderness of your kiss upon my lips as I
allow myself to give this….
Us one more chance….
One more try….
One more time….
for a lifetime
with you…

I choose to make peace with you
To forgive you for trespassing against me
I choose to live life unencumbered by bitterness and
anger
I choose to hear you with an open heart and mind
To listen to and hear the dreams, hopes, desires, pain
and frustration of your life

I choose life….
I choose love over death
I choose victory!

What do you choose?

In the Midst

Lord –
In the midst of the perils of life separated by distance
Overwhelmed with unspoken frustrations
often left perplexed with no answers
and only plagued with more questions

Lord –
In the midst of the storms that blow
Internally and externally
I sit up late at night
Searching for you trying to listen for your voice
His voice

Lord –
In the midst of the deafening silence
Didn't you hear the tearing of my heart as it
disconnected from you... from him

Don't you hear me calling?
Don't you see me wailing?
My heart aches like a rotten tooth
My tormented soul drowns in despair

Lord –
In the midst of the tension
Still waters run deep
Like the roots of a Weeping Willow beside the bank of
a river

So does my love for him
So does my love for you

Why have the storms raged against us?
Why are the winds trying to separate us?
Why have the fiery words burned our hearts and have
only been extinguished by tears?

Lord –
In the midst of all of this where are you?

Sometimes Inspiration

Sometimes Inspiration
        Comes from the most unlikely places
Just listen and hear
        The small quiet voice or feel the wind blow
The breath of inspiration which surrounds you
        The choice is yours
                Whether to embrace inspiration
                        Or run from it

Sometimes Inspiration
        Comes from the most unlikely places
Stop and listen to the birds sing
        Be still and watch the trees sway in the breeze
Rise during the warmth of the day
        And feel the warmth of the sun kiss your skin
Relax under and gaze into the velvety midnight sky as the
stars twinkle
        And the moon glows ever so high

Sometimes Inspiration
        Comes from the most unlikely places
Maybe from a word on a page
        Or even from a glance exchanged between two
lovers
Inspiration can possibly come from something as
simple as a child's laughter
Or an infant's cry or possibly from faded eyes framed
in an elderly

Person's wrinkled face or from the heat rising off city
streets

Just be open to receive your creative encounter
        Unfurl the doors to the abyss of your soul and
allow your mind to unwind
And intertwine with the essence of your being as you
are taken to a higher   plateau

Yield yourself as inspiration ascends from the abyss
and brushes the four corners
        Of your heart and mind which flows into your
fingertips
Write the words that are the residue from your heart
and mind

Let Inspiration have his way like an insatiable lover
allowing him to tickle
Your voice as the words pour over your lips like sticky
honey for only
Those who are around to hear the small quiet voice
speak articulately and succinctly

Sometimes
                Often Times
                        Inspiration comes from the
most

        Unlikely Places

        Embrace It